a book of honest prayers

POWER

William Breault, S.J.

& WEAKNESS

a book of honest prayers

ST. PAUL EDITIONS

Nihil obstat:
  Rev. Msgr. John G. Hogan

Imprimatur:
    ✚ Humberto Cardinal Medeiros
    Archbishop of Boston

  June 29, 1973

Photo Credits:

Robert Dolan, S.J.—pages 12, 14, 18, 20-21, 25,
35, 37, 39, 41, 49, 52, 54-55, 60, 62, 66-67, 68,
70-71, 73, 78-79, 89, 92-93, 98, 102, 115, 118

Daughters of St. Paul—pages 2-3, 26-27, 29, 31,
42, 46-47, 58, 74-75, 80-81, 85, 91, 94-95, 107,
110, 124-125

The Daughters of St. Paul are an international
religious congregation serving the Church
with the communications media.

DEDICATION

To R. Bossenmaier,

who has so generously
helped the author
with catechetical work

CONTENTS

prayer of distraction

Lord,
When I pray
The thought of what I have to do,...
Some future obligation...
Insinuates itself into my mind
And draws me away from You.

But much worse
Is the thought of what I <u>want</u> to do!

For a superficial moment,
I try to hold You in my thoughts;
Then, like some kind of missile,
Aimed with deadly accuracy,
They go, "on target,"
To "what I want."

There seems to be no escape from self,
and what it wants.
But it wants to pray, too!...
This confused and confusing self,
Trying to grapple with the mystery
You are.

So, accept these distractions, Lord.
If I were not trying to reach You...
Or, better, allowing You to reach me,
I wouldn't even experience a distraction!

For they go hand in hand
with my attempt
At inner silence,
My desire to come close to You;
They are more of a pain to me, perhaps,
Than You. □

a prayer

about forgiving

O Lord Jesus,
Help me this day
To forgive...
For I wish to be forgiven:
And I'm afraid
That I can't ask for
What I don't attempt to give.

With You,
I can always come back,
And know
You will receive me,
No matter what my sin is;
Yet I myself
Often put on a hard face
When it comes to
Forgiveness.

Should You do that to me,
I couldn't live;
And certainly I would fear
And deny
Death.

Help me, Lord,
Not to extinguish
The smoking flax,
Not to crush
The bruised reed.
Help me
To see my need
Behind the self-sufficient look
Of those
With whom I live.
Help me, Lord,
To do this
In Your name. □

meadow lark prayer

Oh Lord!
When I look out
At the grass,
And the new spring trees;
And when I hear
The sound, filled with colors,
Of the meadow lark,
I feel a stab of beauty
Mixed with sorrow
That the too-beautiful world
Is passing
Out of my reach!
It's true, Lord, I could look forward
At what is coming to be,
But the passing of what is
Sometimes strikes a more sympathetic note
In me...

For I too,
No matter how forward looking,
Must pass:

Someone will care for me
When I shall become sick
And dependent,
No longer able to exercise
Power
And creative talent!
That which I fought...
The waves I successfully breasted,
The life, from out of which
I carved my own person—
I shall submit to!
Humbly, I hope,
In adoration;
And, as it lays its hand upon me,
I shall shudder
In revulsion,
And anticipation...
Like the cry
Of the meadow lark.
Then, Lord Jesus,
Forgive
And rescue me.
Turn my face forward
At what is coming to be
Forever. □

Lord Jesus,
Each good intention
Not realized;
Each failure
Accepted humbly;
Every contrary happening
And frustration;
Every sadness
And disappointment
Brings us to the edge
of the mystery
of our dependence.
And there we are alone
Before You.
Whatever else this
experience is,
It is personal.

Lord, what is this life
That can be lost so easily,
Disappears so rapidly,
And yet contains so much promise
While we live?

At any moment,
The slender thread
That prevents us from going beyond the edge
Of the mystery
Could be severed!

Nevertheless
We continue to live
On the surface of our lives
As though anchored here
Forever.

Yet there is a vague awareness,
Just below the mirror of the mind
That we live on the rim
Of mystery.

But why do we resist this thought?
Why doesn't it bring about our conversion
To You, Lord Jesus? □

the prayer of terminal disease

Lord!
I plan as though
I shall live forever,
And look into the clouded sky
Thinking of what I shall do
Three weeks from now,
While people close to me
Have already received
Their death sentence
In the form of sickness.

And yet, is my life really so different
From theirs?
Is my "feeling" about it
much more certain
Than theirs?

What makes them
So sorrow-filled,
When they hear
They have a terminal disease?
Don't I also have
A terminal disease?
Or does my refusal
To face that fact—
My ignorance—
Make me feel more certain,
And allow me to function
As though I shall live forever?

Is this the way I close You out?
Denial...
And must I accept
The fact
That I have a terminal disease
Before I can accept You
And the true order
Of reality? □

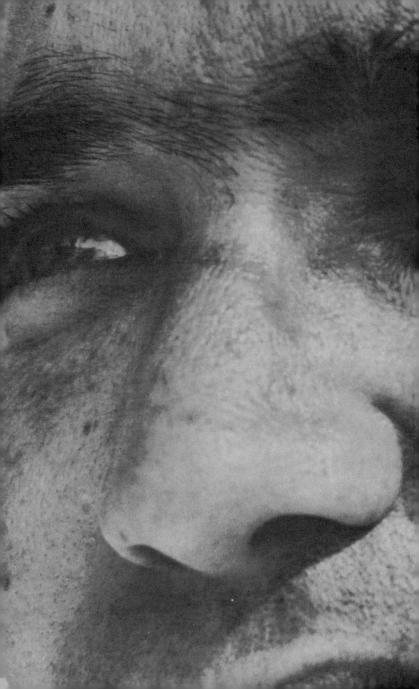

morning prayer

I shall try, this day, Lord,
To love You with my whole heart,
My soul, my body, and my mind.
I shall also love my brother as myself—
At least, I'll try—for love of You,
In him.

Nor will I let failures hinder me,
For I will not be judged
by individual failures, so much
As the whole bent of my life.

I am weak and fearful, Lord;
Easily upset and anxious;

So I will try to live one day at a time,
With the sure conviction
That my future will disclose itself,
When it's time;
For a way will open up, and outward,
And no amount of worry, nor anxiety
Will cause it to happen sooner.

I shall try to discern Your action this way, Lord,
Waiting for it,
Living only this present day:
My worries and concerns, then
Will be limited
By one day.
This way my energies will not be spent
Probing a future I know nothing about....
This act of humility, I believe You ask me:
To trust in the unknown,
And work with the known!

Help me, Lord!
I often fail
And become discouraged;
But Your grace
Can enlighten and bring hope
And purpose...
Above all, peace.
Give me then, Lord, Your grace,
    And Love,
        Your Spirit, and Strength.

                Amen. □

            see Isaiah 30:15-18

a night prayer

Father,
I am tired this evening
Because there were so many things
I should have done
and didn't....
I wasted time
Inflating my ego—
or someone else's
In a mutual back-slapping contest.
How tiring that is!
And how false.

I should have prayed more;
And I could have, too;
I should have listened,
But I talked instead.
I should have directed my thoughts

Toward You
During the day,
Not waiting till the last moment,
Evening.

Still, Father, even now—
Even this late—
The desire to turn my thoughts to You
Is strong,
And rises up from the depths,
Beyond the debris
Of everyday life.

Receive this act
Of trust and love,
Lord,
As I wait for
The little death
of sleep. □

burnt-out prayer

Oh Lord!
The only way I can reach You,
Today
Is on paper.
Life seems so short
And what I have to offer—
Which seems so much,
Potentially—
Actually seems to be so meager
For all the effort I put into it,
So distracted are my aims.
I feel burnt out with taking care
Of useless things...
Or, perhaps just worrying
about useless things.

Instead of taking
each day
For what it is,
I feel
I must compile them
And offer them
To someone,
As a rosary
Of success!

Help me, Lord,
To sift out
What is important
From what isn't. □

prayers of a school

Christ!
I hurt inside
For the boy
Who looks at me
With the cancer
Of distrust
Already beginning to corrode
The pupils
Of his adolescent eyes!

Christ, Son,
Remember the boy
Whose life is a joke:
Four feet tall,
At sixteen!
Not yet aware
Of the fire

teacher

Generating within
By uncomplaining
And ignorant acceptance.

Christ, Son of the Father!
Look
At the black boy
Ashamed of his difference;
Trying to become
A white man—
In his heart angered at him
For making him do it;
Angered at himself
For doing it.

Mercy, Lord. □

a thank-you prayer

I thank You, Lord,
For giving me
The kind of disposition
That forces me to reach upward
Toward You.

Had I never experienced suffering—
Especially the keenest human suffering:
Not getting my own way—
Had I not experienced reversals,
Sickness,
And even a kind of defeat,
I never would have gone outside myself
In search of You.
I would have remained
Imprisoned
Within,
Unaware of my emptiness. □

Mary prayer

Mary!
Mother of God,
Woman, we need you
To help us see
And accept our limitations,
Peacefully,
With that lovely abandonment
So typical of you.

And so silently, fruitfully offered—
Under the pained eye of Joseph,
When his heart's honor was at stake,
And God's honor was infleshed
Within you.

Oh Mary, one of us,
Be close to us.

Teach us to accept
Humbly,
And gracefully
What is good
within us,
And whatever
life sends our way. □

the

prayer of acceptance

"Take this chalice away,"
Were You undecided, Lord,
About Your Father's will?
It doesn't seem so, since You said also:
    "Not my will, but Yours be done."
You saw His will clearly...
Yet, somehow, You also sensed
Within Yourself
The desire for escape.

Could it be that You
Were shrinking from pain and death,
And knowing the Father's will,
Clearly,
Felt that either it must change,
Because of the suffering,
Or You must die
Because of the suffering?

And did Your prayer
Lead You to the point
Of accepting this suffering
And death
As His will...
Did it become, then,
A plea for strength
To carry out His will?

Your prayer in the Garden, Lord,
Like so many of mine,
Does not seem to be
A prayer of decision,
Except to accept
What is already known to be Your will. □

seeing Christ

Dear Christ,
Help me to see You,
Not just on the external,
Social level
When I'm meeting others,
And they, me—but more deeply,
After I've come to know them;

    When I can no longer
    Make excuses for them—

Nor be charmed
    By my own ignorance of them—
    Then, Lord,
    Help me to see

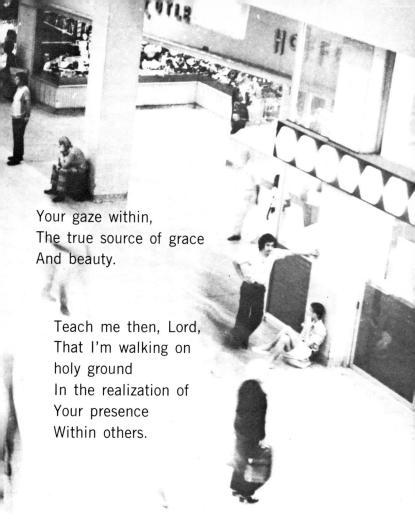

Your gaze within,
The true source of grace
And beauty.

Teach me then, Lord,
That I'm walking on
holy ground
In the realization of
Your presence
Within others.

May respect for the mystery
Of this communion
Grow
Into deep love.

promises

The world, Lord,
Always promises me
more than it gives—
The "biggest sale" in years,
The "finest imported" goods,
The "greatest entertainer"—
A world of superlatives.

I find myself living on "promises"
That never materialize,

And so, I become exhausted with false hope.
I awaken with disgust, confusion,
And a vague sense of guilt
Because I believed the promises
Bombarding my senses.
I hoped for so much,
And realized so little,
So I reach for another promise
To fill the growing vacuum—to stop from thinking.

Your grace, Lord,
Is just the opposite,
Promising a certain hardness
Even opposition,
At first.
Yet surrendering to it
Seems to result in a deep peace
And a free conscience.
It allows me to look at life
With joy.

Teach me, Lord, to forego the promise
Of the "immediate good" and
To discern Your Spirit at work
Within me. □

the scarred Christ

Oh, Christ!
I have this picture of You,
On my desk.
Your right arm is missing
And Your chest is cracked
And flaking away.
The hair is gone from Your head
And heat-blisters
Pock mark Your face...
Victim of an air raid.

Hear me, oh Lord!
Somehow that picture
Sums up all the broken lives
Of the young.
Hear me, Lord,

For all the Michaels
and Cathys...
For all those
Who have so much to say
And no one to say it to—
For those who can't pray,
Hear me, Lord!
For those who live bottled-up lives,
Have mercy on them, Lord Jesus!

Soothe over the deep-grained hurts,
And soften the resentments
That gather over the years.
Take them up,
Into Your scarred and disfigured body
And transform them
As You ascend from death to life. □

sin and weakness

Father,
I see that the only way
Sin can be overcome
Is by that peculiar power
We call weakness,
By goodness,
God-power.

Sin can never be overcome
Except by goodness—never by power.
And that is why
The goodness of people
Floods me with a quiet joy,
Mixed with sadness.
For in their goodness,
I stand revealed to myself.

It took the cross of Your Son:
His goodness, taken advantage of,
To overcome our sin.
And it takes an understanding, forgiving friend
To overcome our own evil.

Show us, Lord,
In Your sacrament—by Your goodness—
How to become more like You,
Forgiving,
Gentle, and filled with joy. □

see 2 Corinthians

56

providence prayer

I wish to live
Guided by You, Lord,
Trusting in Your providence over me—
    I say this when things aren't going well!
    But when they are,
    Then, it seems, I really don't care
    Whether You guide me or not:
    I can handle myself, then,
    In other words.

You're good to have around
When I think I can't make it.
Then, I can make acts of trust,
Knowing that everything that happens
    "Is converted to good
    For those who love you."

But when things are going my way,
I don't have to trust,
I don't have to seek You out
    To explain reversals,
    Nor do I show much gratitude.

Lord, help me to see both,
    The good, and—what looks like—
    The not-so-good,
    As coming from Your hands.

Teach me what gratitude means
    So that I always make a connection
    Between what happens in my life
    And You,
    As Your Son taught us to do. □

a plea for life

Oh Lord God,
Why do we leave
With sadness?
I see that "Good-bye,
I-may-not-see-you-
again" look
In older people's eyes.

Can't we live in peace
And excitement of life,
And still
Leave with joy?
Must death
Always be miserable?
Does it have to lay its hand
On Joy, too?
Turning it into
Pleading?

O Jesus, Son of God!
Save us!
Save all.
Bring us all
To the better life
With You,
Where there is no ending
And life can continue
Without this uncertainty
That constantly threatens it now. □

the prayer of Peter

When Simon Peter saw what had happened,
he fell on his knees before Jesus, and said,
Go away from me, Lord, for I am a sinful man.

see Luke 5:8

God needs help
To bring back the family of man.
In asking for it,
Peter discovers who is asking
And who is asked!

Peter was afraid
For he saw.
He begged the Lord
to leave him:
"Go away from me, Lord."
Did he want the Lord
To do what he asked?
Hardly.
What, then, was he asking?

Others asked the Lord
To leave them,
And He left.
But, here, the Lord
Instead,
Draws Peter into a closer bond.
What, after all,
Was Peter afraid of? □

see Mark 5:17

64

an act of presence

Almighty God,
I place myself
In Your presence
To pray...only I can't this morning!
I'm angry!
And cannot forgive.
I don't even want to forgive—
The injury, after all, was done to me;
<u>My</u> forgiveness should be asked...yet,
I said those words,
Formed in my heart,
With the intention of hurting.
I really wanted
To make the other person smaller,
In his own eyes,...mean, truthful words.
This is what I am angry about.

Oh, Lord!
Don't judge us
By the way we
judge one another,

Or no one
has a chance.

Help me see
How I can be sorry for my anger.
Let me look at that,
And not how I was offended.
Lord, make me at least willing
For a reconciliation,
If I can't reach the point
Of apology. □

a prayer

O Lord!
I can't stand success...
And I work so hard
To insure it,

for those tired people

Driven by the God-Messiah complex:
The compelling feeling
That I must bring solutions
To everyone's world problems.
And so, I spend myself
In a variety of disconnected
And unrelated ways,
And wonder what I have
To show for it.
I would like to run,
But where could I go?
They would follow!—
Since I would remain unchanged
Needing people to want me.
How difficult it is, Lord,
To love,
And still be capable
Of maintaining "distance"! ☐

a prayer

"....If he walks at night he stumbles, because there is no light to guide him."

John 11:10

praising Christ's guidance

Lord,
I trust in Your promise,
In Your guidance
And direction.
Even when I look around me
And see chaos
And destruction...
When nations fall,
And men scan the horizons
Looking for the end
Of their world;
When the earth grows cold
With fear
And mistrust,
Even then I trust in You
And in Your direction;
For You are stronger than the earth,
And You lead man
Through darkness
Toward light,
Even the darkness
Of confusion,
Hatred and sin.
Your love for us, Lord,
Is stronger than death. □

see John 7:12; 9:4-5, 39-41

a morning offering

"...Wisdom is quicker to move than
     any motion;
she is so pure, she pervades and
     permeates all things.
She is a breath of the power of
     God...."
                              Wisdom 7:24-25

Lord,
I wish this day
To live in Your presence;
To be filled
With Your spirit,
So that my thoughts
Touch Yours,
And my words
And actions
Reflect Your goodness,
And flow from You
As a source
And inspiration.

see Psalm 139, Wisdom 7:15-28, Acts 17:23-28; John 15:1-12

the prayer of a sick man

Oh, Father!   Just to live till
tonight

Without plans
for the future,

Not trying to get
anything, therefore...
But rather, living for the moment,
Each moment
And what it brings:

Being grateful for the gift
Of the moment,
Especially for persons,
Yet even for the gift of places,
and meals.
To live in the moment
Now present,

And to savor it fully,
I must become a receiver
Of gifts.
I must learn to listen,
To be receptive.

May You, the giver of all good things,
Work in, on, and through me.
Oh Lord, help me to become pliant
In Your hands;
Not rejecting the gift of myself—
That You have given me—
In senseless anger;
Not fearing
Because something might be denied me
That I feel is essential;
Not anxious,
Since, as You said,
Not one hair of our heads
Is disturbed
But that You know it. □

a prayer for forgiveness

The older brother was so angry that he would not go into the house; so his father came out and begged him to come in.

see Luke 15:28

Lord,
You are my God,
Even when I have sinned
Against You.
Nothing I can do
Can take away this fact.
You are a God of mercy,
Compassion,
And understanding,
Even when I fail
In all three!

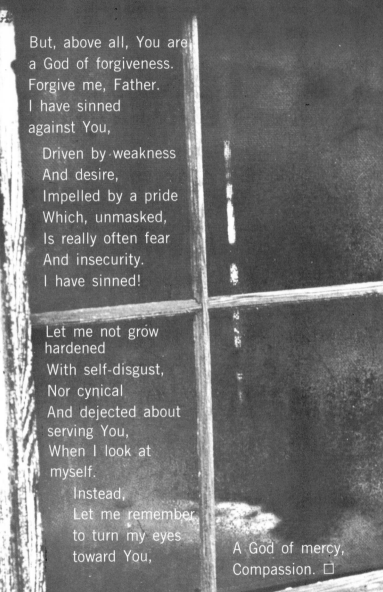

But, above all, You are
a God of forgiveness.
Forgive me, Father.
I have sinned
against You,

Driven by weakness
And desire,
Impelled by a pride
Which, unmasked,
Is really often fear
And insecurity.
I have sinned!

Let me not grow
hardened
With self-disgust,
Nor cynical
And dejected about
serving You,
When I look at
myself.
Instead,
Let me remember
to turn my eyes
toward You,

A God of mercy,
Compassion. □

God is on the side of life

"All who hate me are in love with death."

Proverbs 8:36

What a powerful sentence!
Spoken of God,
And, most especially, of Christ:
God is not on the side of death;
He does not will it,
Nor desire it.
He is on the side of life,
He is life,
Or as John says: God is love.
To hate love,
Or to hate life—they are both the same—
Has the same result: falling in love with death.

And the result is death.
Can one really love death?

Yes, if he hates...
God,
Man,
Or himself.

"Do not court death by the errors of your ways
nor invite destruction through your actions.
Death was not God's doing,
he takes no pleasure in the extinction of the living.
To be—for this he created all;
the world's created things have health in them,
in them no fatal poison can be found...." □

Wisdom 1:12

Prayer: Genesis 4:1-11
        1 John 4:7-12
        John 6:34-40

a prayer of hope

I'm sick, Lord,
Of looking at the negative
In me.
I'm tired of parading
My sins and defects
Before my inner eye.

I'm not even sure
It's a Christian thing to do!

Yes, I fail
Miserably!
But that's not all I do.
I also aspire
Towards not failing!
I want to be good,
Remember.
I want to be useful—perfect!

That's why failure
Is so hard to take;
In fact, Lord,
It seems I'm so fearful of failure
That I forget what I want!
I know what I don't want all right,
But what I do want
Is the important thing, after all:

O Lord!
I want to be free;
I want to be able to respond
To You
Fully.
I want to be young in heart,
Daring all,
Risking life,
Willingly.
I want to be innocent
So that I can see You
Again.

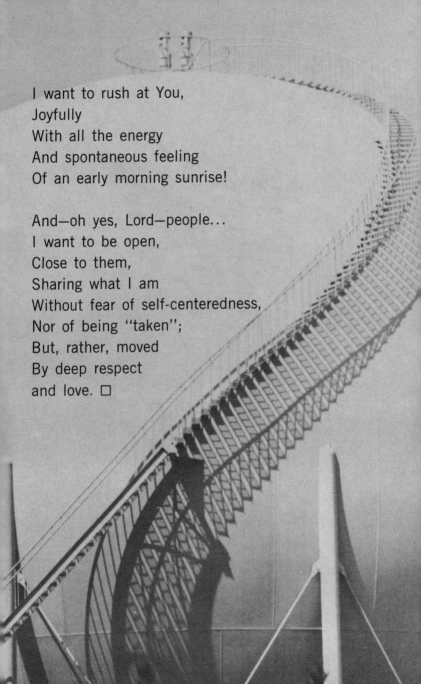

I want to rush at You,
Joyfully
With all the energy
And spontaneous feeling
Of an early morning sunrise!

And—oh yes, Lord—people...
I want to be open,
Close to them,
Sharing what I am
Without fear of self-centeredness,
Nor of being "taken";
But, rather, moved
By deep respect
and love. □

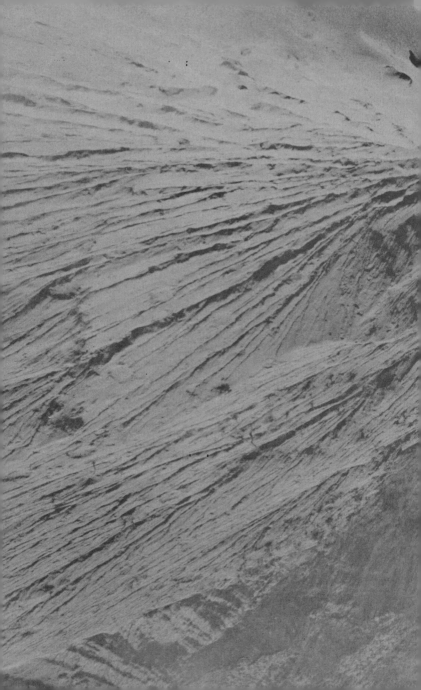

"you know me"

Lord God, it was You who created my inner-
most self
You put me together in my mother's womb.
For this mystery, I thank You.
For the wonder of myself, I thank You.

You know me through and through,
From having watched my bones take shape,
When I was being formed in secret,
knitted together in my mother's womb.

God! How hard it is to grasp Your thoughts!
How impossible to count them.
(I could no more count them than I could the
grains of sand—and suppose I could—even then
You would still be with me.) □

see Psalm 139:13-18

a prayer to listen

O Lord!
I feel tired and depleted,
Burnt out,
Because I talked too much today,
Instead of listening more—
As though I had so much to say,
That if I didn't say it all,
today,
Something great might have been left undone!

Was it really that important, though?
Am I the only one
I listen to?
Indeed! I ask:
Is it possible for me to listen
To someone else?

Especially to the unspoken words
That I see the beginning of,
But cut off
In my rush
To insure silence:
The fitting atmosphere, after all,
For what passes as pearls
From my always-open mouth! □

a prayer for the apathetic

Lord, You are not real
This morning.
My world is much more real
To me;
So I have trouble
Making a connection with Yours.
I am distracted
To the point of dullness,
Glimpsing,
Faintly,
That there are more important things,
But unable to make the effort
To reach them.

Is it always this way, Lord?
Must the "real" world
Always come as Your gift,
Not something I make myself? □

an honest prayer

Oh Father,
You see that we are often
confused about life,
Not knowing which way to turn:
And because of our own desires
And craftiness,
What we want is so often
Opposed to what is
Good for us.
So we resist You.
Hiding in the dark;
Afraid of Your light.
We know You are there, all right,
But we prefer to ignore You
And live as though
This were our only life.
You are gentle,
So You're easy to block out.
Still, Lord, You love
What You have made.
Save us despite ourselves.
We _are_ thick-headed,
But we can be made to see Your truth.
Be patient with our bad moods.
And give us Your light. □ 93

prayer of decision

What a wretched mistake, Lord,
In making decisions
To seek to wrest
From the future
The guarantee of not making a mistake!
Or of not encountering failures,
And the possible consequences
Of the wrong decision.

Such an attitude, Lord,
Paralyzes my spirit,
And reveals
The perversion
Of my basic desire—impossible to fulfill—
To control all life!
To dissect it
And treat it
Like some static, well-preserved
Biological specimen
Capable of being analyzed
In miniature, and
In detail.

Here is man's God-like quality at work,
In its hideous form,
The negative, dark side
Of the dominion handed him
By You, his creator.

Power and knowledge are good,
But without trust, and obedience, and, above all, love
They become destructive. □

a prayer for after anger

Oh Lord,
I grew angry
With You,
But I wouldn't admit it.
Words poured out of my mouth,
Words of pessimism
And condemnation,
One after another,
Each seeking its own share of light,
Till finally I found myself
Asking
You
To damn what stood in my way...
You!
My creator!
The giver of life...
You I asked
To damn life!

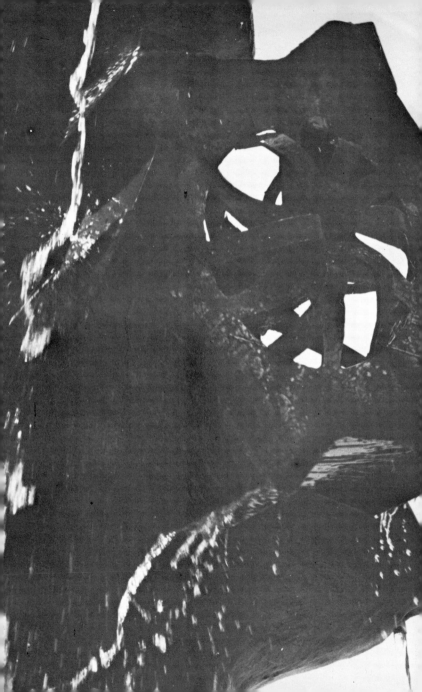

Oh Lord,
Don't pay too much attention to me
When the devil gets his way.
Overlook this sin,
Along with many others.
In my sane moments,
I reject my anger
At not getting what I want—and my desire
Of wanting too much—
And see them as childish.

Do the same, Lord,
And forgive me;
I repent. □

the prayer most of us want

God calls us in our blood.

see Wisdom 7:1-6

To believe
Is to touch God,
And to be touched by God;
After all, someone must call,
Before anyone can respond!
Our response is a desire
To "touch" God.
Once He calls,
We answer,
Below the level of consciousness,
By a certain uneasiness,
The desire to look for meaning,
A search.
"Who called?"

answered

When you stop searching,
You're dead.

Most of us desperately want
The experiences we go through
To mean something
For others—that way,
It means something for us.

Our lives, in other words,
Have their deepest meaning
When shared with others
Somehow.
This is especially true
In the realm of the spirit,
In the hidden struggles with light,
And darkness;
In our struggle with God! □

see Psalm 139

the second world prayer

Lord, I put myself
Into Your presence,
A difficult thing for me to do.
Perhaps, I'm even unwilling
To do it.

Your world and mine
Are different.
Mine is a man-made world,
A hypothesis
Constructed by human reason...
A devastating instrument for destruction,
Without faith!
It says: let us make a world;
And in our world,
Constructed by our reason,
We shall be masters!
Subject to no one!

My world enshrines reason,
The sacred power,
Which looks over all
And decides:
"Let us image ourselves,
Make copies!
Zerox Nature!
And since we shall have excluded God
We shall make our world God....
We created it, after all!"

Then under the mask of holiness
And the desire for truth,
And "sincerity,"
We shall ineffectually beat our fists
On the walls of this "second world,"
Screaming: "There is no God!" and,
"If there were a God, He would rescue us!"

But really,
We don't want to be rescued;
Nor do we want to surrender our world
And stand, stripped of our masks,
Under the gaze of God;
For from Him
We issue.
He
Created us,
And sustains us....
Such a shock, man,
Encoiled in a rational hypothesis
Can hardly bear.

O Lord!
I see this second world in me,
Of my choosing!
Perpetuated by my choosing

And way of acting.
When I cry out to be rescued,
I'm not really sincere;
I mean, instead:
Put my world back together
So I can guiltlessly
Shut You out again.

Your world
Of truth and humility,
And blinding holiness
Haunts
And scares me.
Had I not been introduced into it,
Forcefully,
Unwillingly,
I would have stopped believing in You,
And believed only
In myself.

Only through failure—
A kind different from what I expected—
Did I learn,
Awesomely,
Of Your world.
And of my need.

Save me, Lord,
From my world.
Teach me—and that's no small task!
Teach me what it means
To empty myself out
In love,
As Your Son did for us...
Not all at once, mind You,
But eventually, Lord. □

life and death

"The life and death of each of us
Has its influence on others...."

Romans 14:7

Three things to consider: Each person's life,
And death
Are unique, personal.
Both life—and more importantly, perhaps—
Death
Have meaning;
And both have value for others.

So we shouldn't pass judgment,
For who can judge the value
Of a man's life,
Or death,
Except God? □

a dependence prayer

Lord,
I do not want to accept
The fact
That I am dependent upon You;
Yet that is what I have done,
Verbally,
For years;—in my prayers!
But now, I know it to be true;
Then, I didn't...
It was merely something pious
To whisper,
To convince myself
That I was someone pious!

Now, I know my life depends upon You.
What a shock!

One small blood vessel in my head
Could break,
And my brain
Would be extinguished!
What is it? A gift,
This brain of mine...
Am I that dependent
Upon You?
For my very thought?
Are You at the base of all things,
Giving them being, while all along I thought—
No! I don't like that thought,
It makes me so much like a
Creature,
A created being.
I would much rather

Power and Weakness

I was an uncreated being,
To be honest
With You.
Why, then, do You give me these gifts,
If You're only going to take them away?
O Lord,
Is it that we are not yet fully formed?
Are we still in the embryonic stage,
Wrapped in the womb of time
Waiting for delivery
To join Your first-born?

I feel a certain sense
Of safety,
Security,

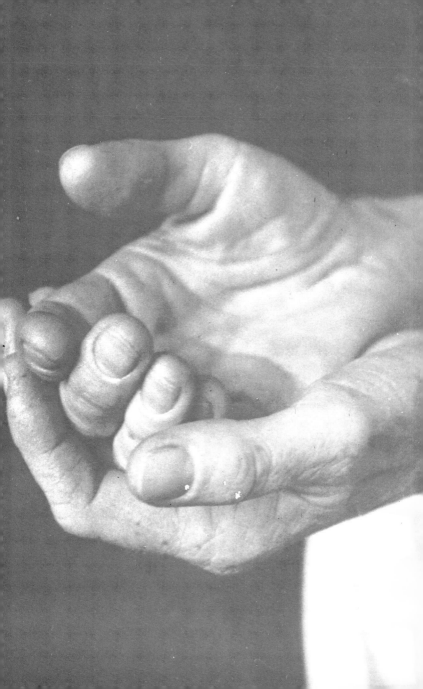

A feeling of solidity
If I can deny You
And the fact that I am created.
Then, I feel liberated,
When I don't have to trace
The source of my being
To You: The universe conceived
And brought me forth,
A unique prodigy.
I am, therefore, responsible to no one!
Indebted to no one!
Free!...yet, also
Absolutely alone,
Too...
For my energy
Was made to rush at its source
In gratitude and love—
Should I turn that on myself?

Can I hope
Through ignorance and denial
To produce what love
And sacrifice
Are meant to do? □

Christ's prayer

What a comfort
To know that the Lord
Had His favorite places
For prayer!
Especially the mountains,
The early morning desert,
And alongside the lake...
But then, also, the garden.
The garden-prayer, though,
Must have been different,
Closed in;
No vistas from on high, there;
A different kind of prayer
from that of the
transfiguration;
The kind that chapter eleven
of Luke's Gospel
speaks about.

I come to You, Father,
In my need—
Which is, perhaps, why You commanded that we pray:
To reveal to us our underlying need,
Our complete and total limitation.
What can we give You, Father,
But this acknowledgment?
This recognition of what binds us to You,
And can become with Your grace
The basis of love. □

see Luke 11:1-13; Matthew 7:7

Daughters of St. Paul

In Massachusetts
   50 St. Paul's Avenue, *Boston*, Mass. 02130
   172 Tremont Street, *Boston*, Mass. 02111
In New York
   78 Fort Place, *Staten Island*, N.Y. 10301
   625 East 187th Street, *Bronx*, N.Y. 10458
   525 Main Street, *Buffalo*, N.Y. 14203
In Connecticut
   202 Fairfield Avenue, *Bridgeport*, Conn. 06603
In Ohio
   2105 Ontario St. (at Prospect Ave.), *Cleveland*, Ohio 44115
In Pennsylvania
   1127 South Broad Street, *Philadelphia*, Pa. 19147
In Florida
   2700 Biscayne Blvd., *Miami*, Florida 33137
In Louisiana
   4403 Veterans Memorial Blvd., Metairie,
   New Orleans, La. 70002
   86 Bolton Avenue, *Alexandria*, La. 71301
In Missouri
   203 Tenth St. (at Pine), *St. Louis*, Mo. 63101
In Texas
   114 East Main Plaza, *San Antonio*, Texas 78205
In California
   1570 Fifth Avenue, *San Diego*, Calif. 92101
   278 17th Street, *Oakland*, Calif. 94612
   46 Geary Street, *San Francisco*, Calif. 94108
In Canada
   3022 Dufferin Street, *Toronto* 395, Ontario, Canada
In England
   57, Kensington Church Street, *London* W. 8, England
In Australia
   58, Abbotsford Rd., Homebush, N.S.W., *Sydney* 2140,
   Australia